ARCTIC OCEAN

Oyashio Current

Bering Current

Alaska Current

North Pacific Current

North Equatorial Current

Labrador Current

North Atlantic Drift

Gulf Stream

NORTH ATLANTIC GYRE

Subtropical Convergence Zone
GREAT PACIFIC GARBAGE PATCH

NORTH PACIFIC GYRE

EASTERN GARBAGE PATCH

California Current

NORTH ATLANTIC GARBAGE PATCH

ATLANTIC OCEAN

Antilles Current

Equatorial Current

Equatorial Countercurrent

Equatorial Countercurrent

South Equatorial Current

PACIFIC OCEAN

SOUTH PACIFIC GYRE

SOUTH PACIFIC GARBAGE PATCH

Peru Current

Brazil Current

SOUTH ATLANTIC GYRE

East Australia Current

South Pacific Current

South Atlantic Current

Antarctic Subpolar Current

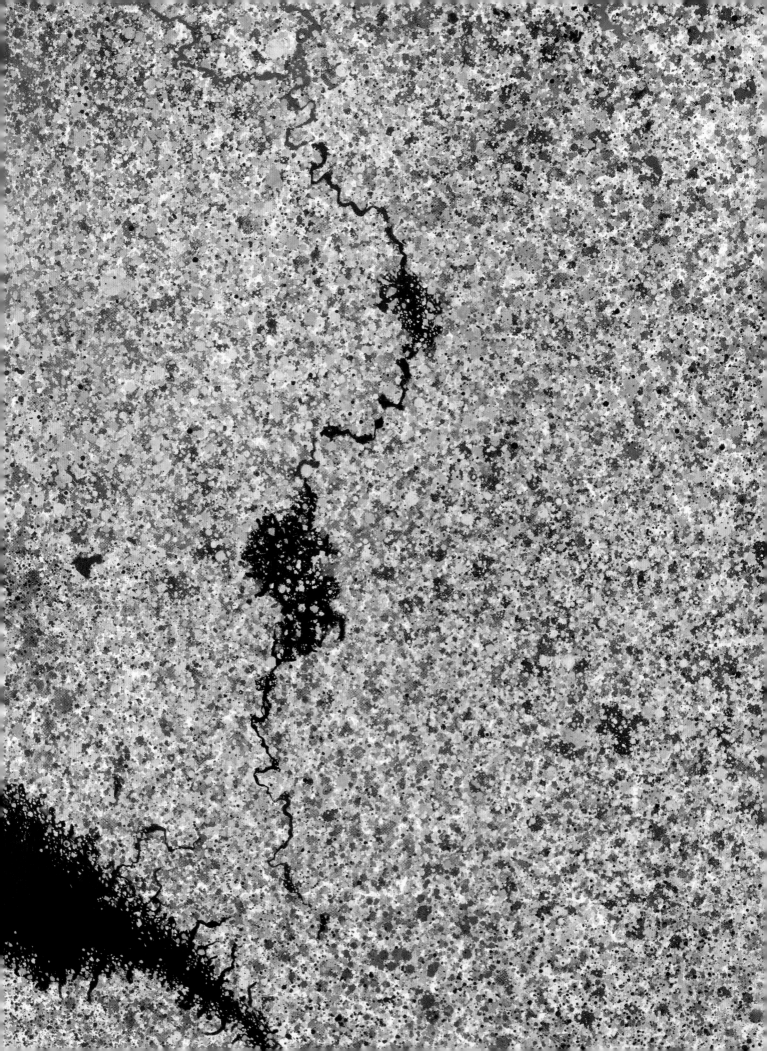

THE NEW OCEAN

The Fate of Life in a Changing Sea

BRYN BARNARD

Alfred A. Knopf • *New York*

The Earth—our home—is covered mostly with water: the wide, deep, salty, and very blue ocean. It regulates our climate in a way that makes life as we know it possible.

This huge ocean is full of an amazing amount of life, most of which is too small to see. We've counted 230,000 species of plants and animals that live in the ocean: from giant whales to phytoplankton (tiny plants) and zooplankton (tiny animals), plus even smaller bacteria, viruses, molds, and fungi. There may be many more, as many as two million different kinds of plants and animals.

Most of the world's oxygen is made in the ocean. The phytoplankton are crucial to its creation. They take the energy of the sun and, through the process of photosynthesis, transform it into oxygen. The ocean churns that oxygen-rich water in majestic, looping currents, mixing oxygen at the surface with water deep below. Ocean life depends on it. Some of this oxygen also turns into the ozone layer, a crucial part of the atmosphere that protects us from the sun's harmful ultraviolet rays.

But life in the ocean is in trouble. The ocean is becoming hotter, more polluted, and, in places, empty of life. As the number of people on our beautiful blue planet has grown, more and more people are burning coal and oil and wood to run electrical plants that heat and light and power our homes, our factories, and our cars. This burning has released billions of tons of carbon dioxide into the air, increasing by nearly half the amount of carbon dioxide in the atmosphere since the start of the Industrial Revolution in 1760. Most climate scientists think this has helped trap the heat of the sun within the Earth's atmosphere, warming the air and the water.

The right amount of warming is good for us, but too much warming is causing changes that are not good for life in the ocean, at least the kind of life that thrives now. Because it is getting hotter, the ice caps are melting and sea levels are rising. If the ice caps melt entirely, as has been the case many times in the distant past, ocean currents and winds may simply stop. The mixing of surface water and deep water that ocean life depends on will cease.

The oceans are also absorbing a lot of the extra carbon dioxide in the air and turning it into acid. This means the ocean is starting to melt the shells of some sea creatures, especially plankton. It is getting harder for these creatures to survive and reproduce. They're disappearing.

Conditions for life in the ocean are getting tougher in other ways. Human beings are dumping billions of pounds of toxic garbage—pollution—into the sea. Plankton eat the garbage, fish eat the plankton, we eat the fish. In effect, we are eating the toxic chemicals we have thrown away. This damages our health and can cause birth defects in our children.

Finally, we have gotten really clever at finding and catching fish, so clever that we are literally emptying the ocean of many kinds of life. Ancient, primitive sea creatures are moving in to fill the vacant spaces. Some of these creatures are poisonous. Some are changing the composition of the very air we breathe.

Taken together, global warming, pollution, acidification, and overfishing are creating a New Ocean, in which life is changing drastically. This book tells the stories of the probable fates of six sea dwellers: jellyfish, orcas, sea turtles, tuna, corals, and blue-green algae—some of the losers and winners in the New Ocean.

What becomes of them may help you understand what may become of us.

Jellyfish are one of the oldest and most successful creatures on Earth. Six hundred million years ago, the Earth was very different from today. It had only one giant, lifeless continent surrounded by a vast sea teeming with life. Jellyfish started in that ancient ocean.

Jellyfish are simple creatures that are made mostly of water. They are round blobs with a mouth, but no brain, heart, or spine. The mouth is surrounded by tentacles and studded with thousands of stinging nematocysts—spring-loaded needles for delivering poison to prey.

• *Jellyfish often eat by waiting for a fish or other sea creature to get entangled in their tentacles, stinging the creature, and then hauling it up to their mouths.*

• *Creatures that eat jellyfish include tuna, swordfish, salmon, and sea turtles. Some people, mostly in Asia, eat jellyfish, too. When dried, they're crunchy.*

• *The lion's mane jellyfish comes in varying sizes but can grow to seven feet in diameter, with tentacles up to 120 feet long—that's as tall as a ten-story building!*

• *There is a species of Australian box jellyfish, the Irukandji, that is only one and a half inches long, about the size of a finger, but its venom is a thousand times more powerful than the bite of a tarantula.*

• *The much larger Australian box jellyfish, or "sea wasp," is considered the most venomous marine creature known. We don't know the total number of deaths caused by sea wasp stings. In Australia, more than sixty deaths have been reported since 1884. But in the Philippine archipelago, where many islands may lack access to antivenin treatments, twenty to forty deaths are reported each year.*

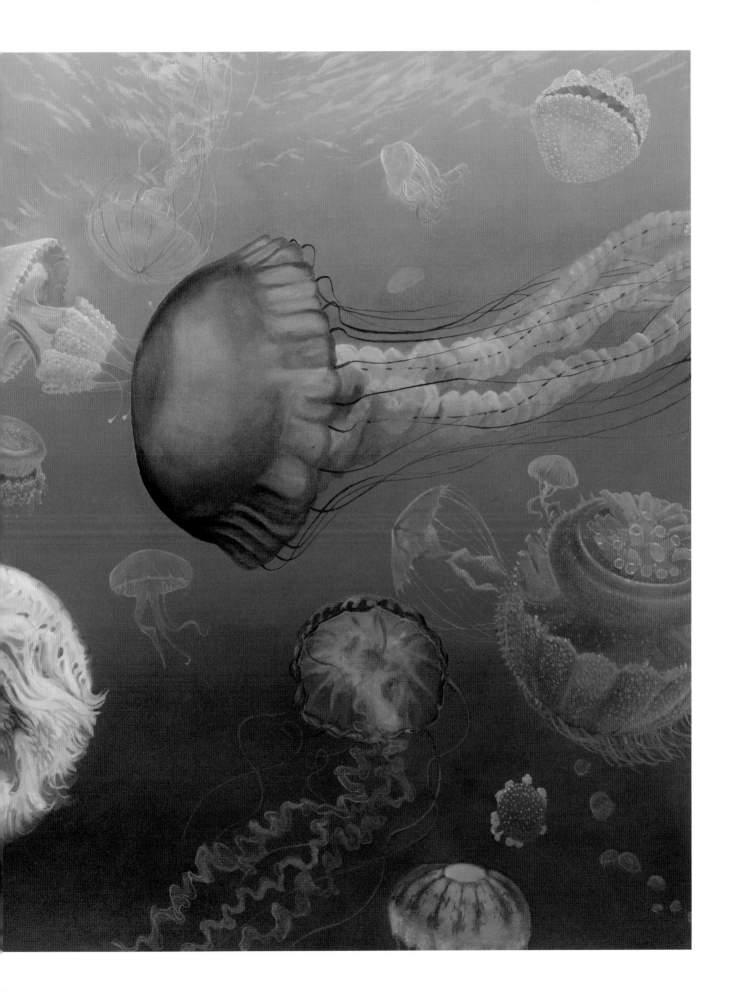

Jellyfish can thrive anywhere. They first evolved in ancient oceans that had little oxygen, and so they can survive today in the ocean's growing dead zones, which have little oxygen and little life. Dead zones are caused by pollution or by changes in the ocean temperature, currents, and wind patterns. These changes stop the mixing of water near the surface (which contains a lot of oxygen) with deep water (which contains less oxygen). Many fish have to avoid these areas. Jellyfish don't.

Jellyfish have also perfected a survival strategy that has allowed them to wait for the ideal time to reproduce. Mature jellyfish produce eggs that sink to the bottom of the sea and grow into polyps: little jellyfish "flowers," with a thin, hollow body and tentacles at one end for catching food. They attach themselves in vast fields to the ocean floor and other hard surfaces. There they wait—for years, if need be—for salinity, temperature, and food to be just right. Then they bud, breaking off bits that turn into thousands of young jellyfish, called medusas. These medusas rise through the water, eating as they go: plankton, baby fish, *everything!* They become the dominant life-form in that part of the ocean. This is called a jellyfish bloom. Blooms can be hundreds of miles wide and consist of millions of jellyfish.

A species of small jellyfish called the immortal jellyfish, which is found in the Sea of Japan and the Mediterranean, is the only known animal that can turn from adult to baby and back again, theoretically forever. As other kinds of ocean creatures disappear, this jellyfish could become one of the ocean's dominant life-forms.

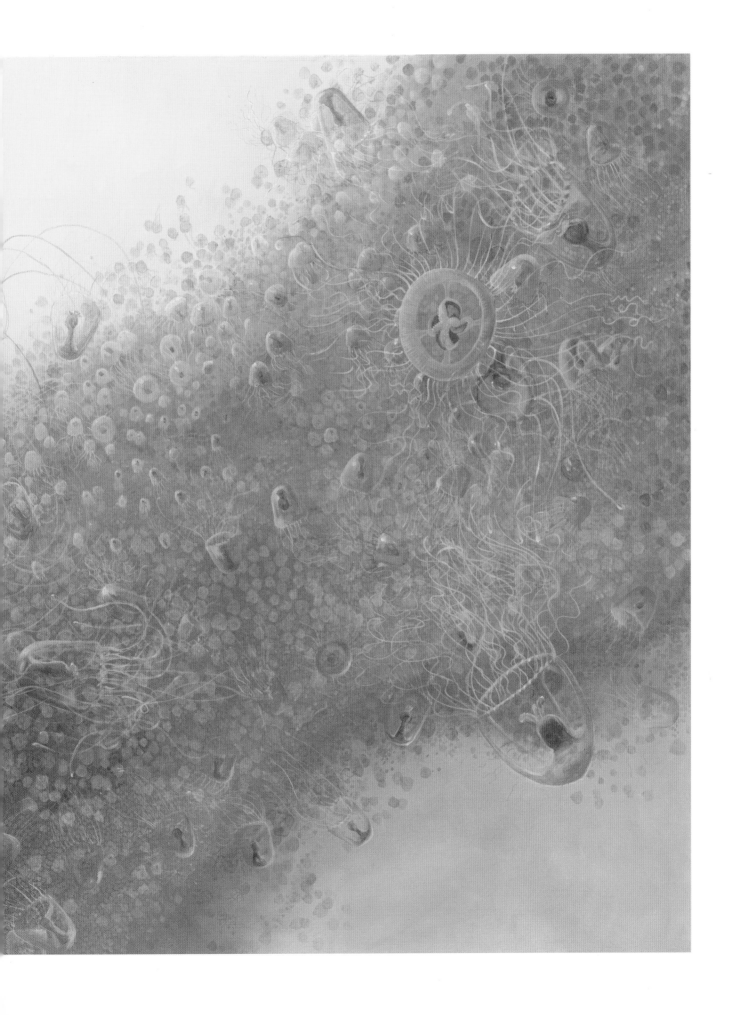

Orcas are whales that live in every ocean of the world. They communicate in long, complex songs of whistles and clicks that mothers teach to their children. Orcas live in tribes called pods, which each sing with different accents—as different as the English spoken in America is from that spoken in Australia. When two orcas meet after having been apart for a long time, they identify one another with special songs. These songs are unique: if an orca becomes lost and separated from its pod, scientists can tell from its song not only the pod to which it belongs but also which orca in that pod is its mother. They also echolocate—project sound waves and read the echoes—to create very precise pictures of the world around them. This helps them to find food.

- *Orcas can hold their breath for up to fifteen minutes, possibly longer, but they have to come up to the surface to breathe air through a hole on top of their head.*

- *Orcas have good eyesight and often pop straight up out of the water to look around. This is called spyhopping.*

- *All orcas have a unique dorsal-fin shape and white or gray saddle patch on their back that can be used to identify them, like a human fingerprint.*

- *Orcas live in close-knit family groups for their entire lives. Some males never leave their mothers.*

Closed Saddle

Offshore Whale

Open Saddle

Resident Whale

Closed Saddle

Transient Whale

Orcas are already considered endangered. Noises like those from motorboats and Jet Skis interfere with echolocation, making it harder for them to find food. Underwater military sonar that allows ships to communicate with submarines is so loud it may actually kill orcas.

Because orcas are at the top of the food chain, they are especially vulnerable to the garbage humans have introduced into the oceans. Everything we pump into the sky and wash into our drains ultimately finds its way into the sea: diapers; waste oil from our cars; billions of particles of nylon, polyester, and other artificial fibers from our clothes; plastic from sandwich bags and toy packaging; mercury from burning coal for electricity; fertilizer to make our grass green. Everything.

All this waste ends up in the ocean, where it works its way back up the food chain to top predators like us. In the simplified illustration at the right, plastics and other garbage produced by people break down into microparticles that are eaten by plankton. Krill (tiny shrimplike creatures) eat the plankton; fish eat the krill; penguins eat the fish; seals eat the penguins; leopard seals eat other seals; orcas eat the leopard seals. At each step, the waste gets more and more concentrated. So by eating a single leopard seal, an orca is getting a dense helping of poison. And orcas eat five hundred pounds of food or so each day. Because of this, orcas, especially resident pods in Puget Sound, are considered some of the most contaminated animals on the planet. Adult orcas aren't living as long as they used to, and many baby orcas are dying soon after being born.

In the wild, orcas can live up to a century. As captives in marine parks, however, they survive on average for only six years, even though in parks they have a steady diet, medical care, and no predators. Why? Orcas have evolved to live in large, complex family units and travel long distances—thousands of miles—to hunt and breed in a rich, stimulating ocean environment. Marine parks often break up orca families. Their tanks are, from the orcas' point of view, the size of bathtubs and about as interesting. As orcas swim around and around in endless circles, their echolocation bounces off the tank walls, sometimes driving them insane. Most captive orcas quickly stop using it, and may simply be dying from hopelessness and boredom.

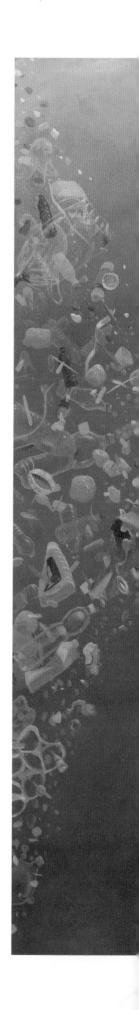

Turtles first appeared 215 million years ago and eventually evolved into about twenty different kinds. Some crawled around on land; others swam about in the sea. Sea turtles became distinct from other turtles 110 million years ago. Most land turtles disappeared in the extinction that wiped out the dinosaurs, but not aquatic turtles, which survived unscathed. Seven species of aquatic turtles survive today. For all but one (the leatherback), their spine and ribs are external and have spread and fused together into a shell called a carapace, which protects them from hungry predators.

Female sea turtles come ashore every few years to lay hundreds of eggs—they dig deep holes in the sand with their flippers, cover the eggs, and then return to the ocean. Kept warm by the sand, the baby turtles peck their way out of their eggs with a special tooth on the end of their beaks. Then they head for the sea—but hungry seabirds and other hunters eat most of them before they reach the water. Only one out of a thousand turtles will survive to adulthood. Those who make it will migrate thousands of miles, and for many years, through the sea.

• *Some ancient turtles were as big and heavy as a modern hippopotamus!*

• *Most sea turtles have a hard carapace, but the leatherback turtle has a soft, rubbery carapace with ridges that allow the leatherback to swim more efficiently than other turtles.*

• *When it is time to first lay their own eggs, sea turtles return to the exact same beach where they hatched.*

• *We don't know the exact life span of sea turtles, but it is long, possibly 150 years or more.*

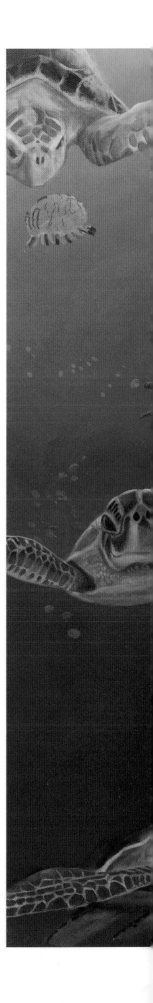

Though sea turtles are tough and resilient creatures, they have not evolved defenses to protect themselves from human beings. Many coastal areas have oil wells that suck petroleum (which we use to make gasoline, plastic, and other products) from beneath the ocean floor. Oil-well accidents can spill millions of gallons of raw petroleum into the ocean, where it can coat thousands of turtles, killing them.

Litter also causes problems. When floating in the ocean, plastic bags can look like jellyfish—a favorite food of sea turtles. Once eaten, the plastic stays inside the turtles' stomachs, taking up space needed for food and blocking digestion, so that the turtles gradually starve to death. Young turtles can also swim into plastic six-pack rings, which can stay on their body for their entire life, slowly warping the shell as the turtle grows.

Turtles also get caught in shrimp fishing nets. Because they are air breathers like us, if they're held underwater for too long, they drown. The United States requires all shrimp nets to use a turtle excluder device (TED)—a trapdoor that keeps the shrimp in but allows turtles to escape. But while TEDs allow smaller turtles to get out, larger turtles, like leatherbacks, perish.

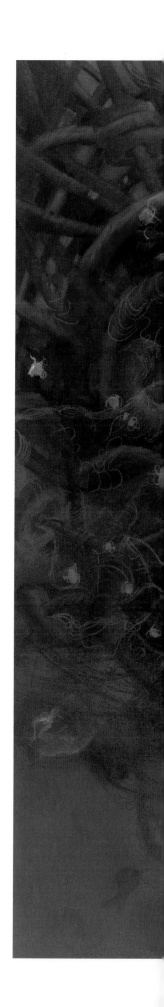

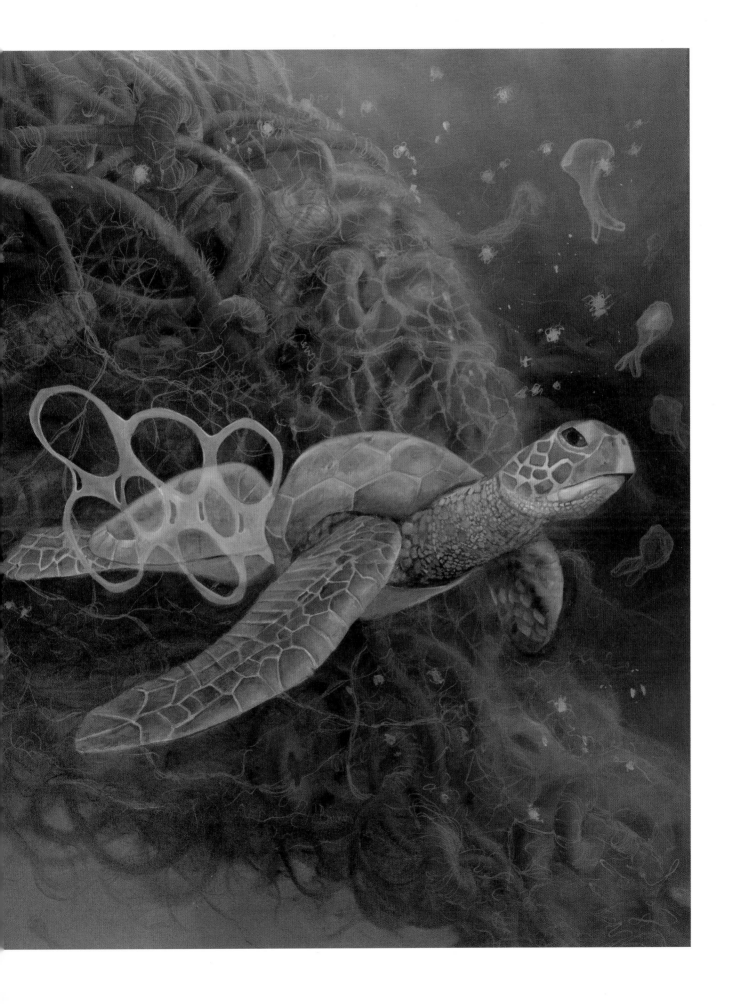

Tuna are some of the fastest fish in the ocean: the word *tuna* comes from an ancient Greek verb, *thyno*, meaning "to rush." They are built for speed, with a rigid head, a torpedo-shaped body, eyes and fins set flush to the surface, and a powerful bony tail. Tuna also have a network of tiny blood vessels under their skin that helps bring oxygen to their muscles so that, uniquely among fish, they have a body temperature that is higher than that of the water around them, allowing them to swim even faster. But they have to swim continuously their entire lives, even when asleep, or else they suffocate. They also have to eat constantly to maintain their energy. They eat eel, mackerel, flying fish, anchovies, squid, herring, starfish, and kelp.

• *Tuna range from the small, foot-long bullet tuna to the massive bluefin, which is longer than a tall human (over six feet) and much heavier (about 550 pounds).*

• *Only one in forty million tuna eggs survive to adulthood, but those that do can live for up to fifty years.*

• *The bluefin swims at nearly fifty miles per hour, and it can go even faster when trying to catch its food.*

• *Bluefins can cross the Atlantic Ocean in sixty days, and many do this several times per year.*

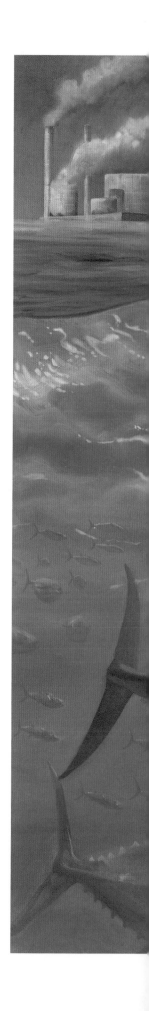

Humans have grown to love tuna—as food, that is. In 1940, humans caught about 300,000 tons of tuna per year. More recently, using a variety of new technologies, we've been able to catch four million tons per year. We have emptied the oceans of fish, virtually wiping out some varieties, especially bluefin tuna. At Japan's famous Tsukiji fish auction, buying the first bluefin of the year is a huge honor. But the price can vary wildly, veering, for example, from $173,000 in 2012 to $1.8 million in 2013 to only $70,000 in 2014. The average price per pound paid to fishermen the rest of the year is much lower, around $15–$25—still enough, it seems, to keep them fishing for bluefin. What will that last fish cost?

If you do eat tuna, beware. All tuna—and, in fact, all fish—contain at least some mercury in their bodies. Mercury falls from the sky in smoke from our coal-fired power plants. This mercury is absorbed by plankton and moves up the food chain to tuna, then to you. The higher on the food chain tuna live, the higher their concentration of mercury. Bluefin tuna, at the very top, has the most.

Even a single six-ounce can of albacore tuna—enough for a tuna sandwich—can push up a person's mercury blood levels. More than two tuna sandwiches a week is too much. Mercury is a neurotoxin—a poison that kills brain cells and makes you unable to control your muscles.

Mercury was once used to make hats, and it drove hatmakers crazy (which inspired the character of the Mad Hatter in *Alice in Wonderland*). Too much mercury can even kill you.

Corals are a group of tiny animals called polyps. Like the polyp stage of jellyfish, these are hollow, cylindrical creatures with a mouth at one end and tentacles used to sting and capture food at the other. They live side by side in a cooperative world we call a reef. They host a special kind of algae that lives inside the polyp. The algae are protected from predators by living inside the corals; in exchange, the algae process energy from the sun and turn it into food the corals can eat.

Together, the polyps and the algae pull calcium out of the seawater and turn it into a mineral called limestone. Depending on the type of coral polyp, these limestone skeletons take on forms that give corals their names, like brain coral, pillar coral, staghorn coral, and orange cup. As generation after generation of coral polyps and algae live, reproduce, and die, the limestone skeletons grow. This is what a coral reef is—a limestone skeleton covered by a thin layer of living coral.

Coral reefs are some of the most diverse ecosystems in the world; they host up to one-quarter of all the creatures in the ocean. Some reefs are small, a few feet across, but some are enormous, like the Great Barrier Reef, which stretches for a thousand miles down the eastern shore of Australia.

A hotter ocean is a problem for corals. They can only tolerate a narrow temperature range. A more polluted ocean is a bigger problem, since this affects corals' ability to get nourishment. But the biggest problem facing corals may be that the ocean is becoming more acidic. Carbon dioxide is a natural part of the air and essential to our survival. It belches out of volcanoes and is exhaled by human beings and other animals. But when carbon dioxide mixes with seawater, it makes carbonic acid, which can melt corals.

There are now seven billion people on Earth, and by the next century, if current trends continue, there will be eleven billion. Each person needs energy for light, heat, and power, and today most of that energy comes from oil and coal. As a result, humans are making too much carbon dioxide too fast, and coral reefs are beginning to simply melt away.

When the ocean becomes too hot or too polluted or too acidic, coral polyps often expel their algae. This event is called coral bleaching, and it is now occurring all around the world, killing coral reefs. If the oceans continue to get hotter and more acidic, within fifty years nearly all the world's coral reefs will die, transformed into bleached skeletons that can support little or no life. The Great Barrier Reef, for example, has lost half its coral in just the last twenty-seven years, and it is expected to lose half of what is left by 2020.

Some scientists are trying to fix the problem by breeding hardier corals that can withstand the harsher conditions of the new ocean. Will they succeed? Maybe.

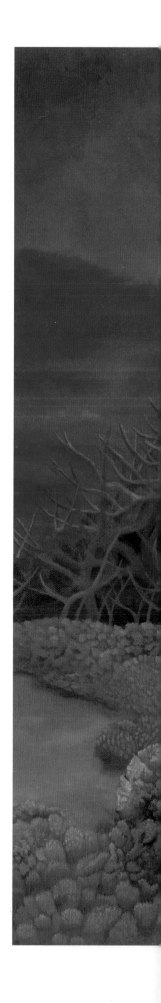

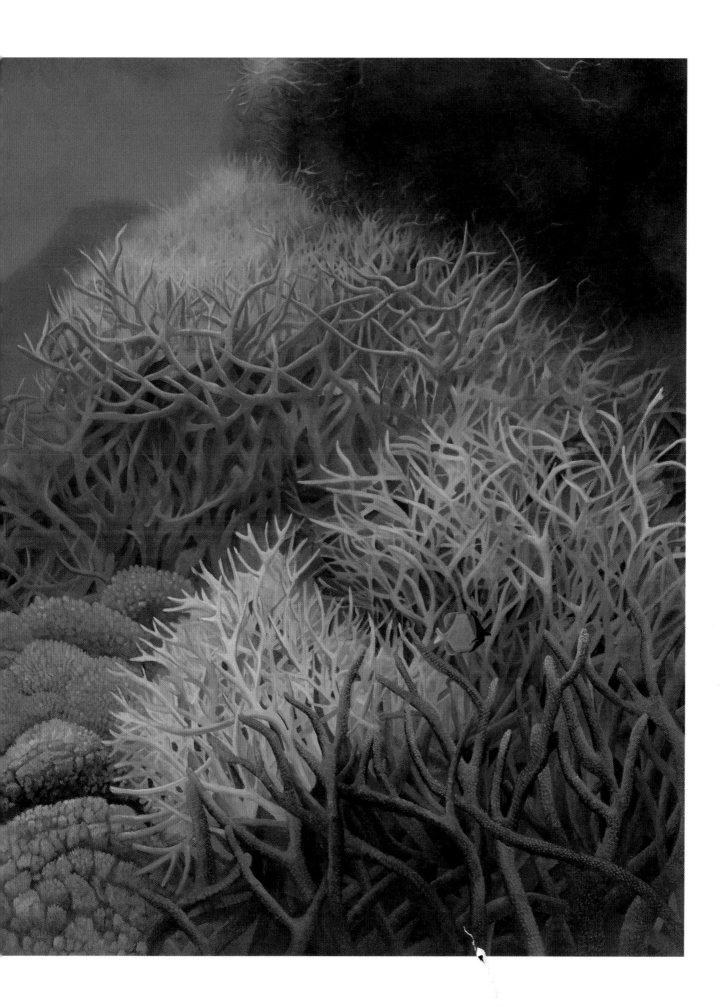

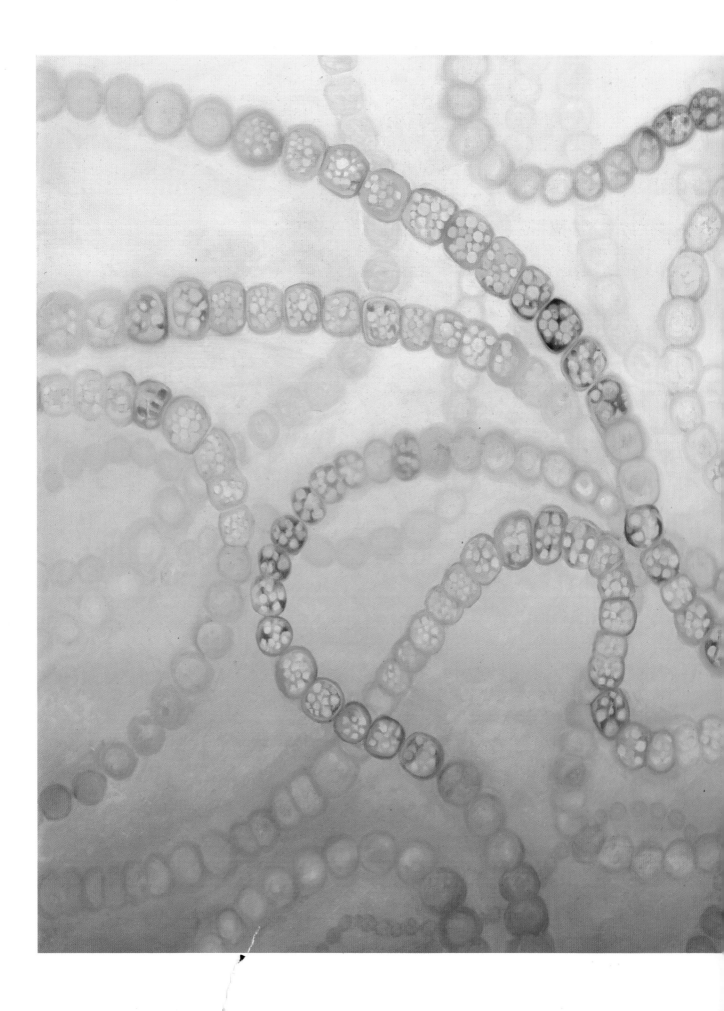

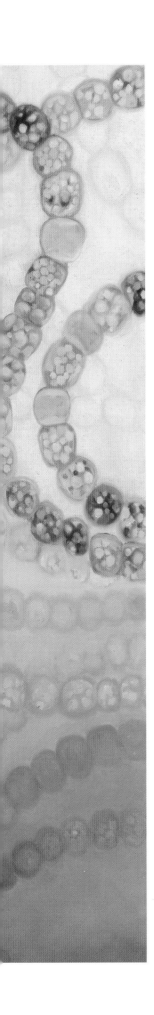

Blue-green algae are one of the oldest and most adaptable creatures on Earth. These microscopic organisms are three billion years old and found everywhere: in the ocean, in lakes, on rocks, in deserts, even in the fur of some sloths, where they work as camouflage.

Blue-green algae are not plants (they are classified as a kind of bacteria), but like plants, they are photosynthetic: they take in sunlight and carbon dioxide and release oxygen. Many sea and land plants make the oxygen we breathe, but blue-green algae were the first to do so. Because of blue-green algae, the ancient Earth's atmosphere changed from one filled with carbon dioxide and other gases to one that is mostly oxygen. Without blue-green algae, the Earth would be a very different place. Because they exist, *we* exist.

• *Many blue-green algae species are toxic, but many others are harmless and taken as a dietary supplement by people who believe it has certain health benefits.*

• *Under certain conditions, blue-green algae can bloom rapidly, like jellyfish can. If toxic, these blue-green algae blooms can kill plants, fish, shellfish, marine mammals, and people.*

• *Despite their name, blue-green algae can come in many different colors. Blue-green algae also come in many structures: as tiny individual cells, as clusters, or as colonies that can form balls or sheets or long strings like dental floss.*

We are filling the ocean with fertilizer runoff, which blue-green algae like to eat, and we are emptying the ocean of fish and other creatures, like sea hares, that eat blue-green algae. Along with jellyfish, blue-green algae are becoming the dominant life-form in parts of the ocean, just as they were three billion years ago. Scientists call this "the rise of slime," a kind of reverse evolution in which the ocean becomes less complex and more like the way it was in the deep past.

As the ocean simplifies, many kinds of blue-green algae are becoming dominant. Fireweed, a stringy blue-green algae found in Australia and Hawaii, contains powerful toxins that cause painful welts if you touch, breathe, or eat it. When conditions are right, fireweed blooms and spreads incredibly fast: up to a football-field-sized patch every hour! Within weeks the blooms cover many square miles, and the toxins kill other sea creatures. When dead fireweed washes up on shore and dries, it can turn into a poisonous, burning powder that can blow far inland, hurting people and animals that eat or breathe it.

As the oceans become warmer and filled with fertilizer nutrients, fireweed is blooming faster than its predators can eat it. Along with jellyfish, blue-green algae like fireweed are returning the ocean to the unfriendly, alien broth it once was long ago.

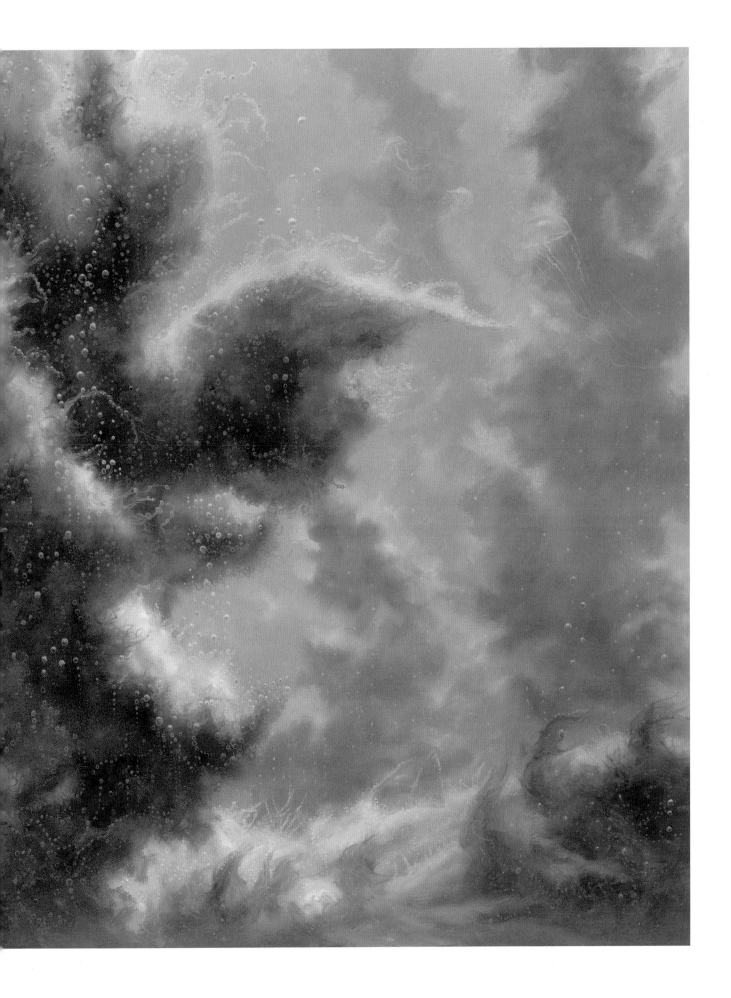

An ocean dominated by jellyfish and blue-green algae may be only the first step in the evolution of the New Ocean. If the climate continues to get hotter, in the next century or so the ice caps will melt, the sea levels will rise, and the oceans will become warm from pole to pole. Most ocean currents will probably stop. The sea may then slowly change into what scientists call a Canfield Ocean, a situation that existed on Earth several times in the ancient past and may have been the cause of many of our planet's periodic mass extinctions.

There have been five great extinctions. Each one took thousands of years to run its course. Each one has killed most life in the sea and on land. After each extinction, it has taken millions of years for the diversity of life to recover and new species to evolve. The last extinction, sixty-five million years ago, killed the dinosaurs and made room for human beings.

In an oxygen-poor Canfield Ocean, ancient bacteria from before the evolution of blue-green algae will take over the sea. Instead of making oxygen, these purple bacteria will photosynthesize rotten-egg-smelling hydrogen sulfide gas, which will tinge the sky green and destroy the atmosphere's protective ozone layer, allowing the sun's deadly ultraviolet rays to penetrate and kill most life.

It may be that with more carbon dioxide in the atmosphere, this climate change is already irreversible. It may be that the human extinction event may actually have begun ten thousand years ago, when people invented agriculture, began clearing forests and jungles for fields, and thus began loading extra carbon dioxide into the atmosphere. It may already have been too late, centuries before you were born. It may be that human beings, like so many species before us, will be just one of those evolutionary experiments that were full of promise at the start, burned brightly, dominated briefly, then flickered out. Some other species may now get its chance to flourish and inherit the Earth.

Or maybe not. Human beings are a "weedy" species, able to survive under many different conditions. We are also clever. It may be that we adapt to a much hotter planet, or that we slow the rise in global temperature, oceanic acidification, and pollution. Scientists are having serious discussions about sending giant orbiting mirrors into space, or using airplanes to pour lots of sulfur into the atmosphere, or building fleets of robot ships to spray mist over the ocean surface, all to reflect

the sun's rays back into space. That won't fix the acid problem or the garbage problem, but it will keep the Earth cooler. For a while.

It might be less risky to let nature regulate the Earth's temperature and to simplify the way we live to keep environmental conditions as they are. You can help. Use less electricity. Drive less. Fly less. Buy less. Use public transportation more. Ride a bike. Walk. Eat local food. Stop using plastic bottles and bags. Eat less fish. And learn as much as you can about the ocean.

Consider the example of Boyan Slat. At age sixteen, this Dutch engineering student was frustrated by all the garbage he encountered while scuba diving. So in 2012, he invented a passive ocean cleaner that uses the ocean's currents to collect plastic garbage. Eventually he led a team of a hundred people to turn his concept into reality. It is such a good idea, he has raised over two million dollars and started a nonprofit foundation. He says that in ten years, half of the Great Pacific Garbage Patch could be collected and removed.

Will you be the next Boyan Slat? You can: Study nature. Study science. Science helps us understand what is happening to the Earth. Science helps us find solutions to problems. Science is our best hope of survival. We need science. We need you.

Sources

Canfield, Donald E. *Ancient Sulfur Biogeochemistry*. Atlanta: Georgia Institute of Technology, 1993.

Dyer, Gwynne. *Climate Wars: The Fight for Survival as the World Overheats*. London: Oneworld, 2010.

Gershwin, Lisa-ann. *Stung! On Jellyfish Blooms and the Future of the Ocean*. Chicago: University of Chicago Press, 2013.

Greenberg, Paul. *Four Fish: The Future of the Last Wild Food*. New York: Penguin Press, 2010.

Hohn, Donovan. *Moby-Duck: The True Story of 28,800 Bath Toys Lost at Sea and of the Beachcombers, Oceanographers, Environmentalists, and Fools, Including the Author, Who Went in Search of Them*. New York: Viking, 2011.

Intergovernmental Panel on Climate Change. "Climate Change 2013: The Physical Science Basis," 2013. *ipcc.ch/report/ar5/wg1/*

Kennedy, Paul. "Moby Doll," April 8, 2014. *cbc.ca/ideas/episodes/2014/04/08/moby-doll-1/*

Kirby, David. *Death at SeaWorld: Shamu and the Dark Side of Killer Whales in Captivity*. New York: St. Martin's Press, 2012.

Leonard, Annie. *The Story of Stuff: How Our Obsession with Stuff Is Trashing the Planet, Our Communities, and Our Health—and a Vision for Change*. New York: Free Press, 2010.

Moody, Skye. *Washed Up: The Curious Journeys of Flotsam and Jetsam*. Seattle: Sasquatch Books, 2006.

Narula, Svati Kirsten. "Sushinomics: How Bluefin Tuna Became a Million-Dollar Fish." *The Atlantic*, January 5, 2014. *theatlantic.com/international/archive/2014/01/sushinomics-how-bluefin-tuna-became-a-million-dollar-fish/282826/*

Smith, Rick, and Bruce Lourie. *Slow Death by Rubber Duck: How the Toxic Chemistry of Everyday Life Affects Our Health*. Toronto: Vintage Canada, 2009.

Spotila, James R. *Sea Turtles: A Complete Guide to Their Biology, Behavior, and Conservation*. Baltimore: Johns Hopkins University Press, 2004.

Thorne-Miller, Boyce, and John Ctena. *The Living Ocean: Understanding and Protecting Marine Biodiversity*. Washington, DC: Island Press, 1991.

Van Oppen, Madeleine J. H. *Coral Bleaching: Patterns, Processes, Causes and Consequences*. New York: Springer, 2009.

Ward, Peter D. *The Flooded Earth: Our Future in a World Without Ice Caps*. New York: Basic Books, 2010.

———. *The Medea Hypothesis: Is Life on Earth Ultimately Self-Destructive?* Princeton: Princeton University Press, 2009.

———. *Under a Green Sky: Global Warming, Mass Extinctions of the Past, and What They Can Tell Us About Our Future*. New York: Smithsonian Books/HarperCollins, 2007.

Weiss, Kenneth R. "A Primeval Tide of Toxins." *Los Angeles Times*, July 30, 2006. *articles.latimes.com/2006/jul/30/local/la-me-ocean30jul30*

Glossary

albacore a species of tuna, the only kind that can be marketed as "white meat tuna" in the United States.

algae a diverse group of cellular organisms that can live alone (unicellular) or in groups (multicellular). The cells are eukaryotic, meaning they have a nucleus with a membrane. In the oceans, the most complex kinds of algae are seaweeds. Most algae are photosynthetic.

bacteria microscopic, single-celled organisms. They are prokaryotic, meaning their nucleus has no membrane. Bacteria were among the earliest living things on Earth. In terms of total mass, they collectively outweigh all plants and animals combined.

bluefin the largest, fastest, and most valuable species of tuna. Extraordinary ones can weigh 550 pounds!

blue-green algae a diverse group of aquatic cellular organisms that can live alone or in groups. They are more properly called cyanobacteria, and being prokaryotic, they are not actually algae, nor are they necessarily blue-green. They are the earliest-known oxygen-producing organisms on Earth.

Canfield Ocean a kind of anoxic (oxygen-free) and sulfidic (full of sulfur) ocean theorized by geologist Donald Canfield that occurred several times in the past and may have led to some of the Earth's periodic mass extinctions.

carapace the hard portion of a turtle's shell that protects its back. It also refers to crustacean shells, such as those of crabs and lobsters.

carbon dioxide a naturally occurring chemical compound composed of two oxygen atoms bound to a single carbon atom, and often referred to by its chemical formula: CO_2. Carbon dioxide exists on the Earth mostly as a gas, at a rising concentration in the atmosphere of 407 parts per million as of 2016. Plants, algae, and blue-green algae use CO_2 to photosynthesize food, producing oxygen as a by-product. In 1760, at the beginning of the Industrial Revolution, atmospheric CO_2 was 280 parts per million.

chlorophyll the green pigment found in blue-green algae, algae, and plants that allows them to convert sunlight into energy.

coral bleaching the condition in coral reefs whereby coral polyps, under extreme environmental stress, expel the photosynthetic algae they depend on to turn sunlight into food. The algae give coral its coloration. After the algae are expelled, the coral becomes light or white. If stressful conditions persist and the algae are unable to return, the coral dies.

echolocation the biological sonar (biosonar) used by several kinds of animals, including orcas. These animals navigate their environment by producing sound waves and then listening for the resulting echoes from the various objects nearby.

fireweed a kind of toxic blue-green algae that grows on seagrass and that, upon contact, causes serious skin irritation in people and other animals.

fungi a eukaryotic family of organisms that help decompose dead plants and animals. Some are also parasites, living off the energy of other creatures.

hydrogen sulfide a colorless gas produced by some anaerobic bacteria that has the smell of rotten eggs and is corrosive, flammable, and explosive.

mass extinction an event characterized by the widespread and rapid disappearance of living species. It's believed that 98 percent of all species that have ever lived are now extinct, though they die at uneven rates. Most die in mass extinctions, of which there have been five, occurring, respectively, 65, 200, 251, 375, and 450 million years ago. Extinctions can last decades, centuries, or thousands of years. Many scientists believe that we have now entered a sixth mass extinction.

medusa the adult, free-floating, umbrella-shaped stage of the jellyfish life cycle.

mercury the only metallic element that exists in a liquid state at room temperature. Mercury is found in many rocks, including coal, and is released into the atmosphere when coal is burned. Humans exposed to large amounts of mercury or its compounds can suffer mercury poisoning, which causes difficulties in seeing, hearing, speaking, feeling, and coordination.

mold a type of fungus that grows in the form of multicellular filaments.

nematocyst a tiny hollow capsule containing a coiled, poisoned, explosive barb used by jellyfish, anemones, and corals to ward off enemies and capture prey.

neurotoxin a poison that targets the nervous system.

oxygen the third most abundant element in the universe, making up about 20 percent of the Earth's atmosphere. Normally, two oxygen atoms link up (O_2).

ozone an unstable version of oxygen made up of three oxygen atoms (O_3). This pale blue gas has a strong, pungent smell. In the high atmosphere, ozone absorbs harmful ultraviolet radiation, helping to protect plants and animals.

photosynthesis the process in which blue-green algae, algae, and plants convert sunlight into chemical energy.

phytoplankton microscopic creatures, also known as microalgae or "plants of the sea," that contain chlorophyll and require sunlight to live. They are the base of the marine food chain and produce more than half of the world's oxygen.

polyp an organism with a soft, tube-like shape and a mouth surrounded by tentacles. Living coral reefs are made up of millions of individual polyps. It is also one stage of the jellyfish life cycle.

sea hare a large sea slug whose rounded shape on the ocean bottom looks like a rabbit. Sea hares eat fireweed. In Australia, when sea hares wash up on land, they collapse and are referred to as beach blobbies.

spyhopping the whale and dolphin version of treading water. The cetacean floats vertically, its head above the water, for sometimes minutes at a time, enabling it to survey its surroundings.

turtle excluder device (TED) a special apparatus that allows sea turtles to escape from a fisherman's net. TEDs are an effective way of keeping turtles out of nets, even though larger turtles, like leatherbacks, are too big for TEDs and cannot escape. Since sea turtles have lungs and need to breathe air, if they cannot get free, they will drown.

ultraviolet light electromagnetic radiation with a frequency that is shorter than visible light but longer than X-rays. Ultraviolet light can alter the chemical bonds in molecules and thereby damage living things. It causes suntan, sunburn, and skin cancer.

virus an ultra-microscopic, non-living, infectious agent that can only replicate inside other living cells.

zooplankton tiny animals that live all or part of their lives near the surface of the ocean, feeding on phytoplankton. They form a vital component of the marine food chain.

ACKNOWLEDGMENTS

I grew up in Southern California by the edge of the Pacific, spent many years on the Indian Ocean, raised my family on an island in the chill waters of the Salish Sea, learned to scuba-dive in the Arabian Gulf, and now live on the Sea of Japan. Along the way, many people helped me appreciate our dependence on the ocean for our survival, too many to enumerate here. But I am especially grateful to the late Ben White, whose fearless activism in protecting marine mammals inspired me to write this book; to Dr. Peter Ward of the University of Washington for reading an early draft of the manuscript; to my editor, Michelle Frey, for believing in this project and guiding my writing and research; and to my art director, Isabel Warren-Lynch, for encouraging me to write illustrated books in the first place and giving shape and beauty to this design. Finally, I'm appreciative of the work of Kelly Delaney, who helped craft the text; Nicole Gastonguay, who helped create the design; and Artie Bennett, Alison Kolani, and Janet Renard, who ensured that my facts, grammar, and spelling are so much more precise and accurate than I could possibly make them on my own. To all of you: thank you.

For Wynn and Parks

THIS IS A BORZOI BOOK PUBLISHED BY ALFRED A. KNOPF

Copyright © 2017 by Bryn Barnard

All rights reserved. Published in the United States by Alfred A. Knopf, an imprint of Random House Children's Books, a division of Penguin Random House LLC, New York.

Knopf, Borzoi Books, and the colophon are registered trademarks of Penguin Random House LLC.

Visit us on the Web! randomhousekids.com

Educators and librarians, for a variety of teaching tools, visit us at RHTeachersLibrarians.com

Library of Congress Cataloging-in-Publication Data is available upon request.
ISBN 978-0-375-87049-1 (trade) — ISBN 978-0-375-97049-8 (lib. bdg.) — ISBN 978-0-307-97403-7 (ebook)

The text of this book is set in 13-point Goudy Old Style.
The illustrations were created using oil on canvas. The maps were created in Adobe Photoshop.

MANUFACTURED IN CHINA
May 2017
10 9 8 7 6 5 4 3 2 1

First Edition

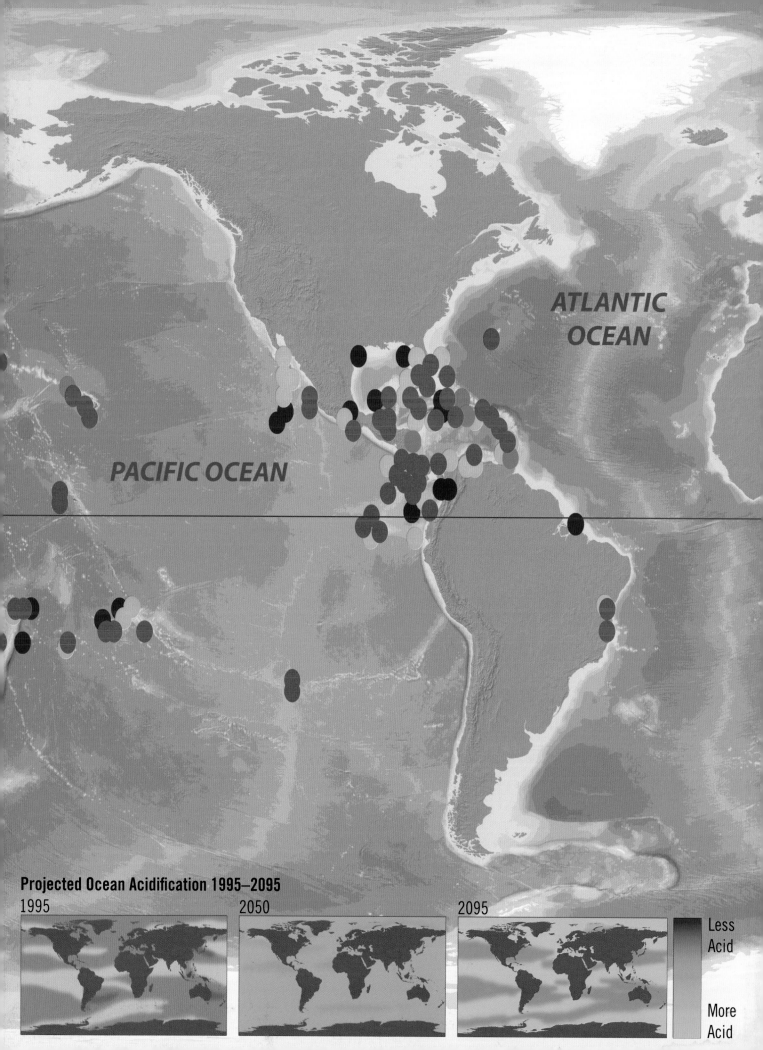

ATLANTIC OCEAN

PACIFIC OCEAN

Projected Ocean Acidification 1995–2095

1995   2050   2095

Less Acid

More Acid